CHARLOTTE HORNETS

ALL-TIME GREATS

BY STEPH GIEDD

Book design by Jake Slavik
Cover design by Jake Slavik

Photographs ©: Chuck Burton/AP Images, cover (top), cover (bottom), 1 (top), 1 (bottom), 12; Chris O'Meara/AP Images, 4; Ruth Fremson/AP Images, 6; Nick Wass/AP Images, 9; Travis Bell/The Herald/AP Images, 10; Pat Sullivan/AP Images, 14; Tony Gutierrez/AP Images, 16; Chris Szagola/AP Images, 18; John Minchillo/AP Images, 20

Press Box Books, an imprint of Press Room Editions.

ISBN
978-1-63494-660-5 (library bound)
978-1-63494-684-1 (paperback)
978-1-63494-731-2 (epub)
978-1-63494-708-4 (hosted ebook)

Library of Congress Control Number: 2022919958

Distributed by North Star Editions, Inc.
2297 Waters Drive
Mendota Heights, MN 55120
www.northstareditions.com

Printed in the United States of America
Mankato, MN
082023

ABOUT THE AUTHOR

Steph Giedd is a former high school English teacher turned sports editor. Originally from southern Iowa, Steph now lives in Minneapolis with her husband, daughter, and pets.

TABLE OF CONTENTS

BOGUES
1
CHARLOTTE
1
Magic
3

CHAPTER 1
ORIGINAL HORNETS

The Charlotte Hornets played their first NBA season in 1988–89. Point guard **Muggsy Bogues** was there from the start. Bogues stood 5'3". He was the shortest player in NBA history. But he made up for his lack of height. Bogues was quick and an excellent passer. No player in team history had more assists than Bogues.

Shooting guard **Dell Curry** played alongside Bogues for nine full seasons in Charlotte. They ended their careers as the two leaders in games played in team history.

Curry was an elite scorer off the bench. In 1993–94, Curry was the Sixth Man of the Year. That honor is given to the best bench player each season. Much of his scoring came from behind the three-point line. Curry made 41 percent of the three-pointers he took with Charlotte.

The Hornets picked **Larry Johnson** with the first pick in the 1991 draft. The forward lived up to the hype that comes with being a top pick. Johnson averaged a double-double his first season in the league. That earned him the Rookie of the Year Award in 1991–92. Johnson followed that up by scoring 22 points per game in his second season. That's how he made one of his two All-Star teams. Johnson was known for strength and big dunks. He used that strength to average more than 19 points per game with Charlotte.

Center **Alonzo Mourning** made an impact right away in 1992–93. He was a force on offense and defense in the paint. Mourning averaged more than 21 points per game in his three seasons in Charlotte. He averaged more than three blocks per game, too. Mourning and Johnson helped lead the Hornets to their first 50-win season in 1994–95.

The Hornets traded Mourning after the 1994–95 season. They got forward **Glen Rice** in return. Like Mourning, Rice played in Charlotte for three seasons. Rice made the most of them. He was an All-Star all three years. He shot 44 percent from deep with the Hornets. That helped him average 23.5 points per game.

STAT SPOTLIGHT

POINTS PER GAME IN A SEASON

HORNETS TEAM RECORD

Glen Rice: 26.8 (1996-97)

CHARLOTTE
41
RICE
41

CHARLOTTE
14
MASON
14

Rounding out the late 1990s roster was big man **Anthony Mason**. "Mase" was a consistent player who averaged a double-double for the Hornets. His big frame made him a physical defender as well.

Mason and Rice led the Hornets to back-to-back playoff appearances in 1996–97 and 1997–98. They beat the Atlanta Hawks in the opening round in 1998. But Charlotte never went further than that.

BEATING THE BEST

The Hornets had a 20–62 record in their first season. But they had at least one game to be proud of. On December 23, 1988, Chicago Bulls legend Michael Jordan played his first professional game in North Carolina. That's where Jordan grew up. The Hornets spoiled his homecoming, though. They defeated the Bulls 103–101.

50
OKAFOR
50

CHAPTER 2
TEAM IN TRANSITION

Charlotte went through a big change in the early 2000s. The Hornets moved to New Orleans after the 2001–02 season. But the NBA didn't stay away from Charlotte for long. In 2004–05, the Bobcats arrived as Charlotte's new NBA team.

The Bobcats took **Emeka Okafor** second overall in the 2004 draft. The big man was

STAT SPOTLIGHT

CAREER REBOUNDS

HORNETS TEAM RECORD

Emeka Okafor: 3,516

voted Rookie of the Year in 2004–05. He used his 6'10" frame to grab a lot of rebounds. Okafor averaged a double-double all five seasons he played for Charlotte.

Forward **Gerald Wallace** was the main star for the Bobcats. He annoyed opponents

BECOMING THE BOBCATS

The NBA's New Orleans team was called the Hornets in 2004–05. So Charlotte's new team needed a new name. Owner Bob Johnson chose "Bobcats." There are plenty of bobcats in North Carolina. And Johnson wanted his team to play with the ferocity of a bobcat. Charlotte became the Hornets again in 2014 after New Orleans became the Pelicans.

with his tough defense. Wallace led the league with 2.5 steals per game in 2005–06. He also led the Bobcats to their first playoff appearance in 2009–10.

Charlotte fans already knew **Raymond Felton** before the team drafted him in 2005. He led the University of North Carolina to a championship that year. Felton always looked for open teammates. He led the Bobcats in assists in four out of his five seasons with the team. But Charlotte was about to watch an even better point guard.

HORNETS
15
WALKER
15

CHAPTER 3
BUZZ CITY

Charlotte drafted one of the team's greatest players in 2011. The team was built around point guard **Kemba Walker** for almost a decade. Walker stood only 6'0". But he created shots with his dribbling skills. Walker was at his best in the clutch. His late-game heroics earned him the nickname "Cardiac Kemba." And he consistently got better in Charlotte.

STAT SPOTLIGHT

CAREER POINTS

HORNETS TEAM RECORD

Kemba Walker: 12,009

Walker scored a career-high 25.6 points per game in 2018–19. That was his last season with the Hornets.

Joining the team two years after Walker was 6'11" center **Cody Zeller**. "The Big Handsome" made the All-Rookie team in 2013–14. Zeller made more than half of the shots he took in his eight seasons with Charlotte.

THE G.O.A.T. GOES HOME

Michael Jordan grew up in North Carolina. And he won a championship with the University of North Carolina before joining the NBA. In 2010, Jordan bought the Charlotte Bobcats for $275 million. As an owner, Jordan helped bring the name "Hornets" back to Charlotte.

The Hornets got two players from the Boston Celtics that made an impact. Charlotte traded for shooting guard **Terry Rozier** in 2019–20. "Scary Terry" was an offensive force. He scored more than 18 points per game for Charlotte. The Hornets traded for

HORNETS
2
BALL
2

Gordon Hayward a year after Rozier. The small forward could light it up from distance. He made 40 percent of his three-pointers in Charlotte. And he averaged more than 17 points per game.

The Hornets took **LaMelo Ball** third overall in the 2020 draft. At 6'7", Ball was bigger than most point guards. That size helped him shoot over opponents. And it helped him find open teammates. Ball's great offensive skills earned him the Rookie of the Year Award in 2020–21. In his second season, he made the All-Star Game after averaging more than 20 points per game. Charlotte fans had hope that Ball could be the one to bring a title to Buzz City.

TIMELINE

1988
1990
MUGGSY BOGUES
(1988-97)
DELL CURRY
(1988-98)
ALONZO MOURNING
(1992-95)
LARRY JOHNSON
(1991-96)
GLEN RICE
(1995-98)
ANTHONY MASON
(1996-2000)
2000
EMEKA OKAFOR
(2004-09)
GERALD WALLACE
(2004-11)
RAYMOND FELTON
(2005-2010)
2010
KEMBA WALKER
(2011-19)
CODY ZELLER
(2013-21)
TERRY ROZIER
(2019-)
2020
GORDON HAYWARD
(2020-)
LAMELO BALL
(2020-)
2023

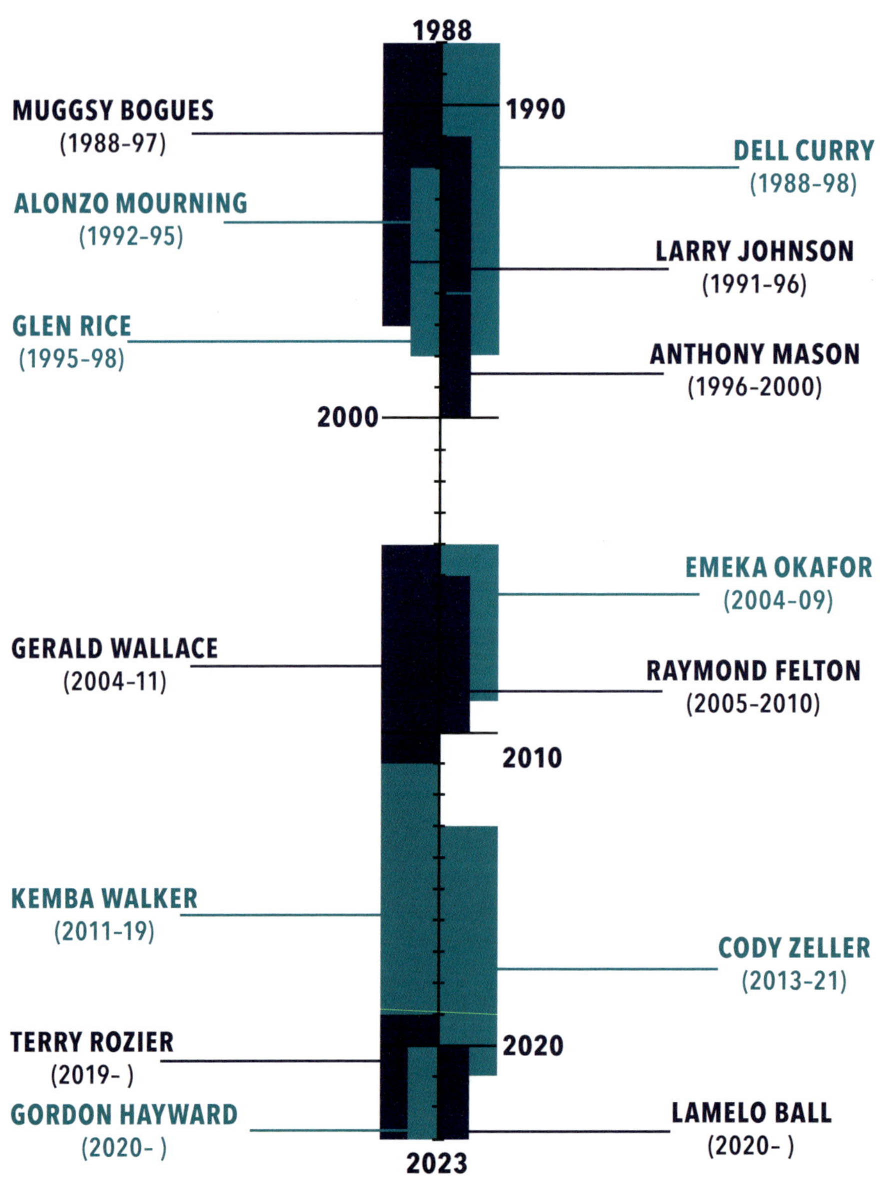

TEAM FACTS

CHARLOTTE HORNETS

Team history: Charlotte Hornets (1988–89 to 2001–02; 2014–15 to present), Charlotte Bobcats (2004–05 to 2013–14)

First season: 1988–89

NBA championships: 0*

Key coaches:

Allan Bristow (1991–92 to 1995–96)
207–203, 5–8 playoffs

Dave Cowens (1996–97 to 1998–99)
179–109, 4–8 playoffs

MORE INFORMATION

To learn more about the Charlotte Hornets, go to **pressboxbooks.com/AllAccess.**

These links are routinely monitored and updated to provide the most current information available.

**Through 2021–22 season*

GLOSSARY

assists
Passes that lead directly to a teammate scoring a basket.

clutch
An important or pressure-packed situation.

consistent
Reliable, unchanging.

double-double
A game in which a player has double-digit numbers in two categories.

draft
An event that allows teams to choose new players coming into the league

elite
The best of the best.

paint
Another term for the lane, the area between the basket and the free throw line.

rookie
A first-year player.

INDEX